D1172193

Australian Animals

Wombats

By Sara Louise Kras

Reading Consultant: Gail Saunders-Smith, PhD

Content Consultant: Bob Cleaver, owner
Wombat Rise Sanctuary, a home for rescued Australian wildlife
Sandleton, South Australia

Capstone
press

Mankato, Minnesota

Pebble Plus is published by Capstone Press,
151 Good Counsel Drive, P.O. Box 669, Mankato, Minnesota 56002.
www.capstonepress.com

Books published by Capstone Press are manufactured with paper
containing at least 10 percent post-consumer waste.

Library of Congress Cataloging-in-Publication Data
Kras, Sara Louise.
Wombats / by Sara Louise Kras.
p. cm. — (Pebble plus. Australian animals)
Includes bibliographical references and index.
Summary: "Simple text and photographs present wombats, their physical features,
where they live, and what they do" — Provided by publisher.
ISBN 978-1-4296-3313-0 (library binding)
ISBN 978-1-4296-3872-2 (pbk.)
1. Wombats — Juvenile literature. 2. Endemic animals — Australia — Juvenile
literature. I. Title. II. Series.
QL737.M39K73 2010
599.24 — dc22
2008050537

Editorial Credits
Jenny Marks, editor; Bobbie Nuytten and Ted Williams, designers; Svetlana Zhurkin, media researcher

Photo Credits
Alamy/Brian Elliott, 11; Dave Watts, 19
Getty Images/DEA/C. Dani – I. Jeske, 9; The Image Bank/Bob Stefko, cover, 5
Nature Picture Library/Dave Watts, 15
Peter Arnold/Doug Cheeseman, 17
Shutterstock/Johnny Lye, 13; Liv Falvey, 7; Robyn Butler, 21; Timothy Craig Lubcke, 1

Note to Parents and Teachers

The Australian Animals set supports national science standards related to life science. This
book describes and illustrates wombats. The images support early readers in understanding
the text. The repetition of words and phrases helps early readers learn new words. This book
also introduces early readers to subject-specific vocabulary words, which are defined in the
Glossary section. Early readers may need assistance to read some words and to use the Table of
Contents, Glossary, Read More, Internet Sites, and Index sections of the book.

Table of Contents

Living in Australia

Wombats are shy marsupials that live in Australia. Wombats look like small bears.

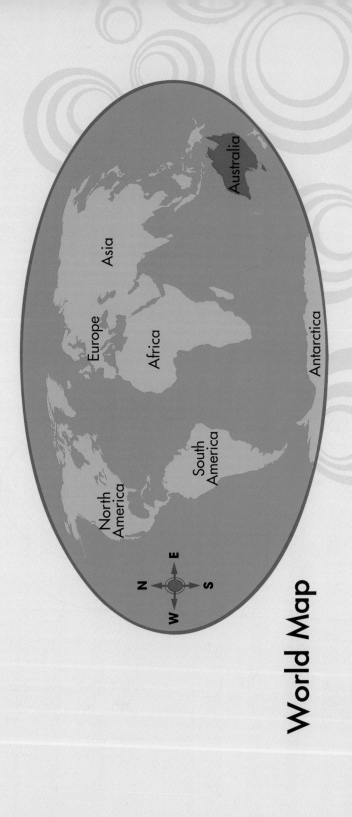

World Map

Wombats live only in Australia.

They dig burrows beneath forests and dry grasslands.

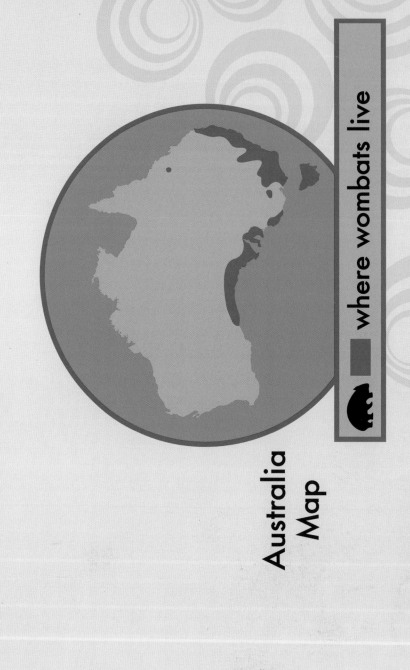

Australia Map

where wombats live

Up Close!

Wombats have short legs
and furry bodies.

They weigh up to 90 pounds
(41 kilograms) and are
4 feet (1.2 meters) long.

Wombats have a split top lip.

Their four front teeth are sharp.

Wombats can tear and eat plants

that grow close to the ground.

Eating and Sleeping

During the day wombats sleep
at the ends of their tunnels.

They often lie on their backs
with their feet in the air.

At night wombats come out

of their burrows to eat.

They munch on fresh grass

and tree roots.

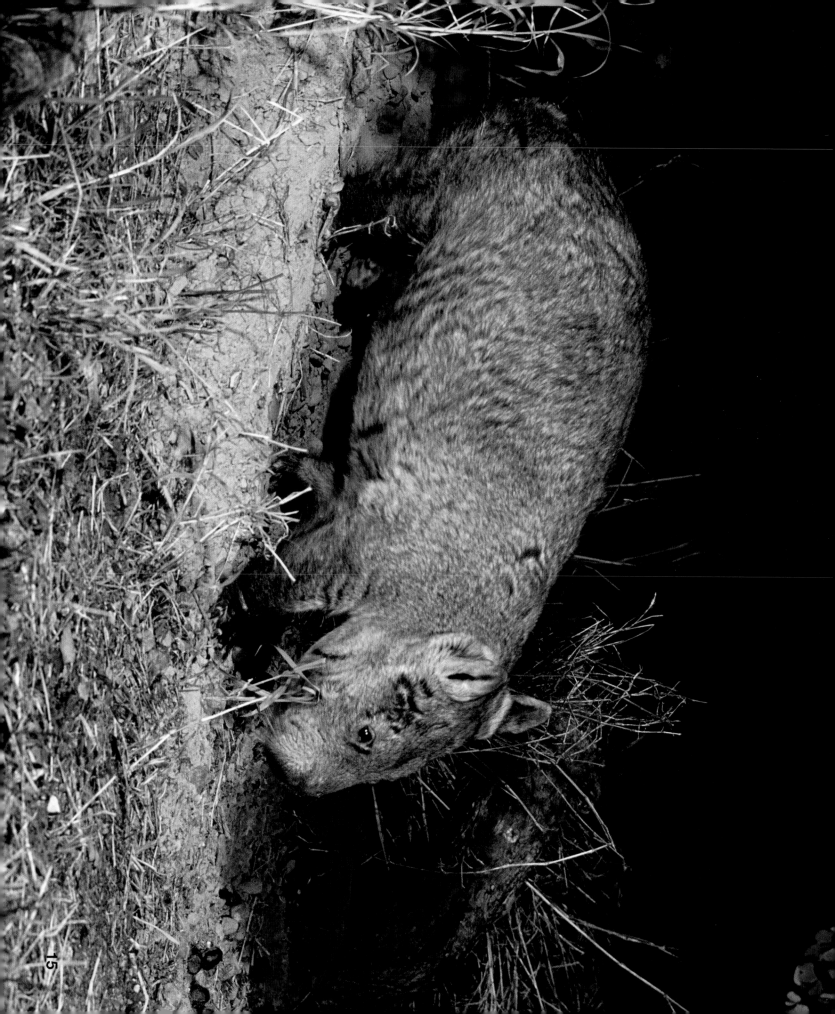

Life Cycle

Female wombats have
one joey every other year.
The joey lives
in its mother's pouch
for about six months.

Staying Safe

Predators like eagles and foxes

try to eat young wombats.

Wombat mothers protect

their joeys from danger.

Some wombats
are endangered.

The wombats and their homes
are being protected.

Laws keep the wombats safe.

Glossary

burrow — a tunnel or hole in the ground made or used by an animal

endangered — at risk of dying out

grassland — a large, open area where grass and low plants grow

joey — a young wombat

marsupial — an animal that carries its young in a pouch

pouch — a pocketlike flap of skin

predator — an animal that hunts other animals for food

protect — to guard or keep safe from harm

root — the part of the plant that is underground

Read More

Arnold, Caroline. *A Wombat's World.* Caroline Arnold's Animals. Minneapolis: Picture Window Books, 2008.

Kras, Sara Louise. *Kangaroos.* Australian Animals. Mankato, Minn.: Capstone Press, 2009.

Sill, Cathryn. *About Marsupials: A Guide for Children.* Atlanta: Peachtree, 2006.

Internet Sites

FactHound offers a safe, fun way to find Internet sites related to this book. All of the sites on FactHound have been researched by our staff.

Here's all you do:
Visit www.facthound.com

FactHound will fetch the best sites for you!

Index

Word Count: 166
Grade: 1
Early-Intervention Level: 24